For James – AL
For Dana Bergstrom – CT

'I felt as though I'd been plumped on
another planet, into another geologic
horizon of which man had no knowledge
or memory.' ADMIRAL RICHARD E. BYRD, 1938

Alison Lester and Coral Tulloch

INTO THE ICE

REFLECTIONS on ANTARCTICA

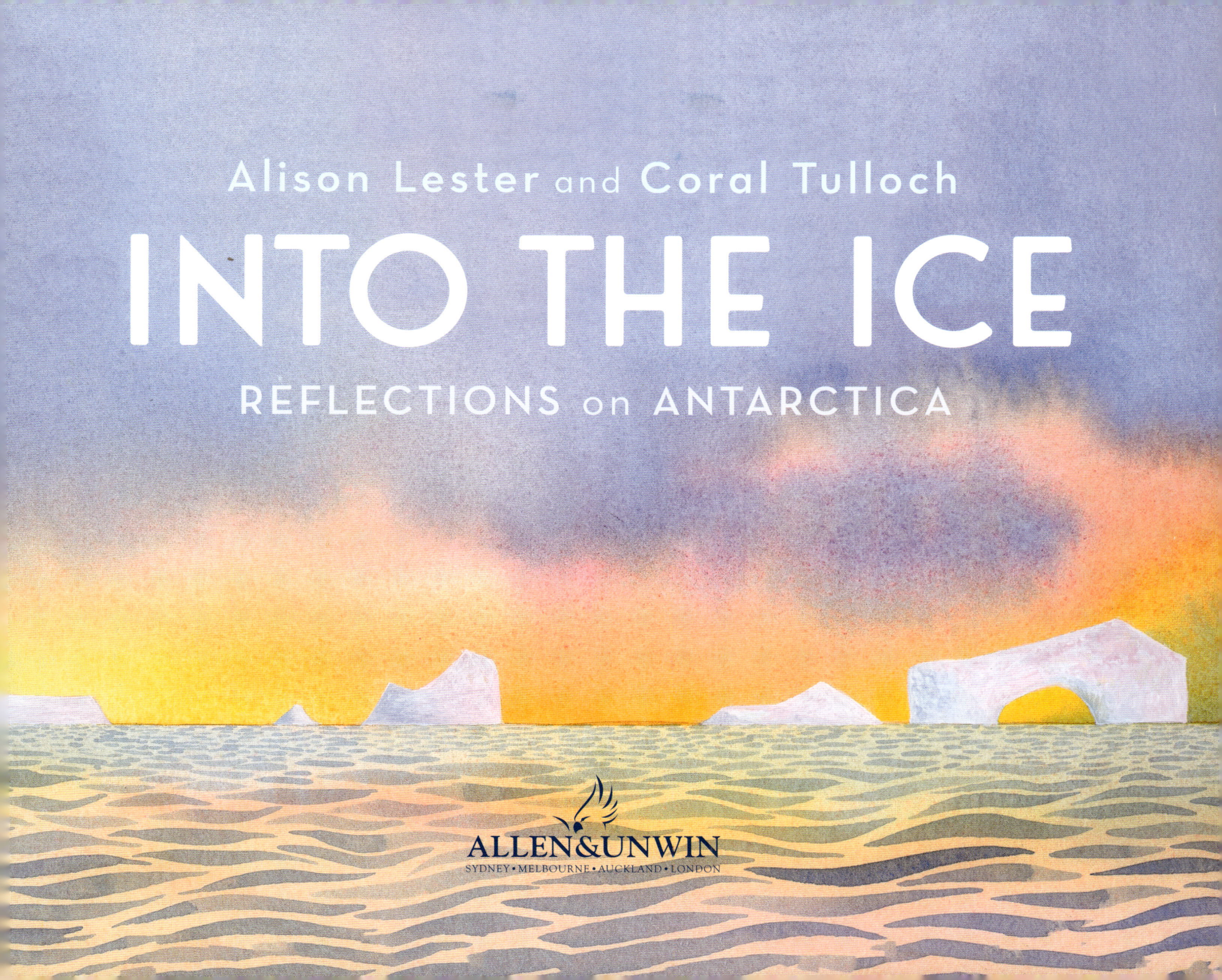

ALLEN&UNWIN
SYDNEY · MELBOURNE · AUCKLAND · LONDON

We have visited Antarctica many times, first as Arts Fellows with the
Australian Antarctic Division, and later on expedition ships taking tourists south.

Antarctica inspires people to create incredible things and share the wonder of the continent with the world.

This book takes you on a southern journey, beginning with a massive storm we both experienced.
We share some of our own reflections along with images and stories from people we
admire. We hope you will be inspired and your curiosity will lead to a greater
understanding and care for this extraordinary place.

Everyone is changed in some way by visiting Antarctica. Some say once you go, you will always
have ice in your veins, and that there is a spiritual bond that exists between all who voyage south.

Let us lead you into the ice…

Alison Lester and **Coral Tulloch**

I was excited and scared at the same time. Excited to be travelling so far, for so long, across some of the wildest ocean on Earth with a team of strangers. I wasn't the mother, wife, cook anymore, I was the artist. That alone gave me a giddy happiness, just being an individual after decades of family life.

I was also worried. It was so remote where we were going. If the ship got into trouble, we'd be too far away for rescue. My friend Rob, a ship's master for decades, told me to be prepared. 'Count the steps from your bunk to the cabin door, then to the exit. Make sure you memorise this, because if you need to get out quickly THE SHIP MIGHT BE UPSIDE DOWN!'

The ship looked huge beside the wharf but later, when we were in the Southern Ocean, she felt tiny. It took all day to be ready, but finally we moved away from the city and headed into the darkening night, leaving behind everything that was safe and familiar. **AL**

'The sea, washing the equator and the poles, offers its perilous aid, and the power and empire that follow it ... "Beware of me," it says, "but if you can hold me, I am the key to all the lands."' RALPH WALDO EMERSON, 1860

6

A **massive storm** stretches across the Tasman Sea and into the Southern Ocean. It follows us with patches of intensity so large, they swirl and end in a teardrop of black isobars above the Balleny Islands – where we are headed.

One morning we wake, caught in the eye of the storm. Ice floes on the ocean's surface heave and roll, pushed by the deep swells below. A force 11 gale fractures their 8–10 metre height with roads of open ocean. I quickly draw the bow of the ship as it's dwarfed by the rolling ice.

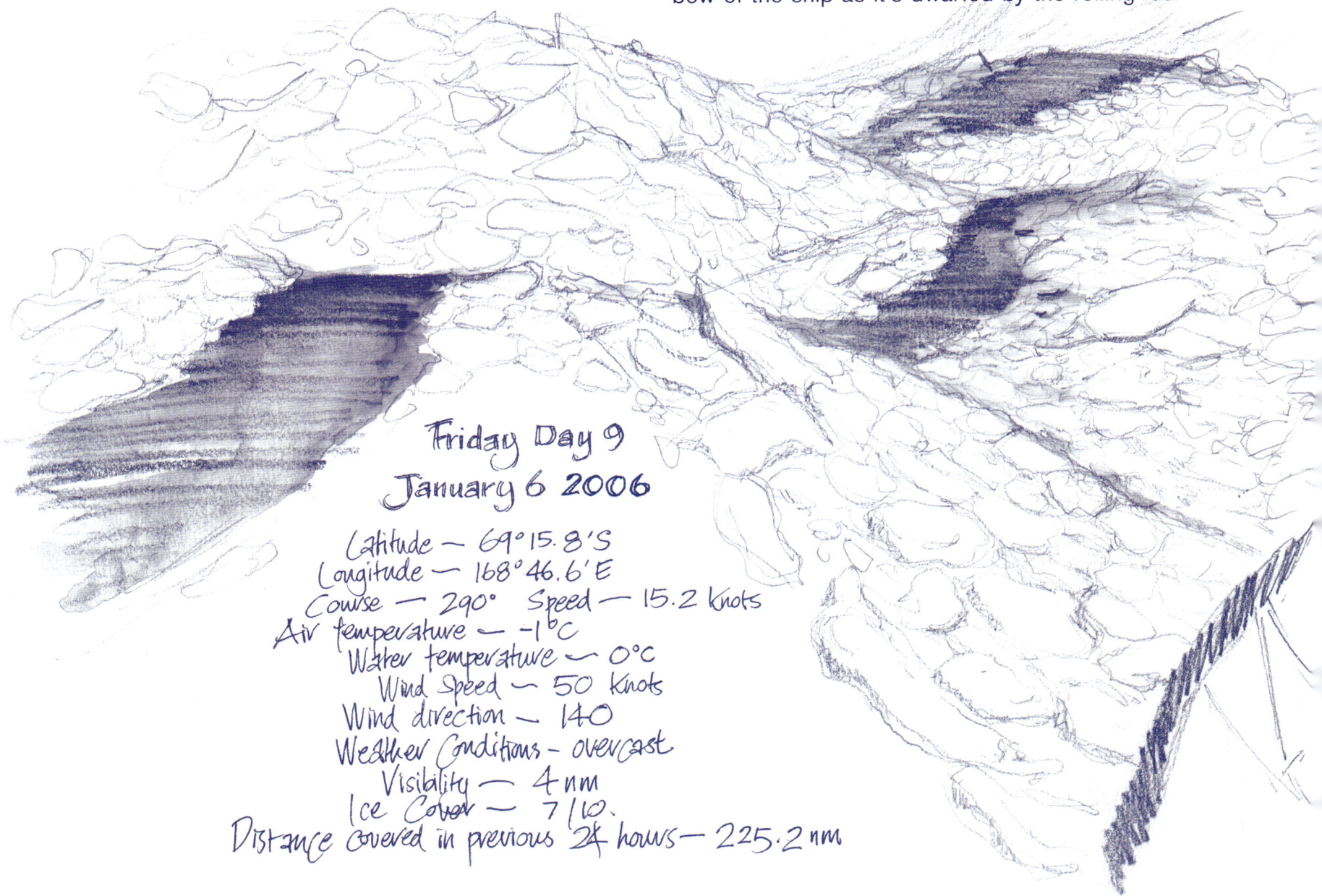

Friday Day 9
January 6 2006

Latitude — 69° 15.8' S
Longitude — 168° 46.6' E
Course — 290°   Speed — 15.2 knots
Air temperature — -1°C
Water temperature — 0°C
Wind Speed — 50 knots
Wind direction — 140
Weather Conditions - overcast
Visibility — 4 nm
Ice Cover — 7/10.
Distance covered in previous 24 hours— 225.2 nm

The ship pitches, picking up mountainous blocks of ice that fly around the bow and decks, defying their weight. The six engines of this massive icebreaker strain against the battering. The captain must try to save the ship and us all.

The only safety is to find dense pack ice, and smash a forceful home, wedging the ship into metres of solid ice.

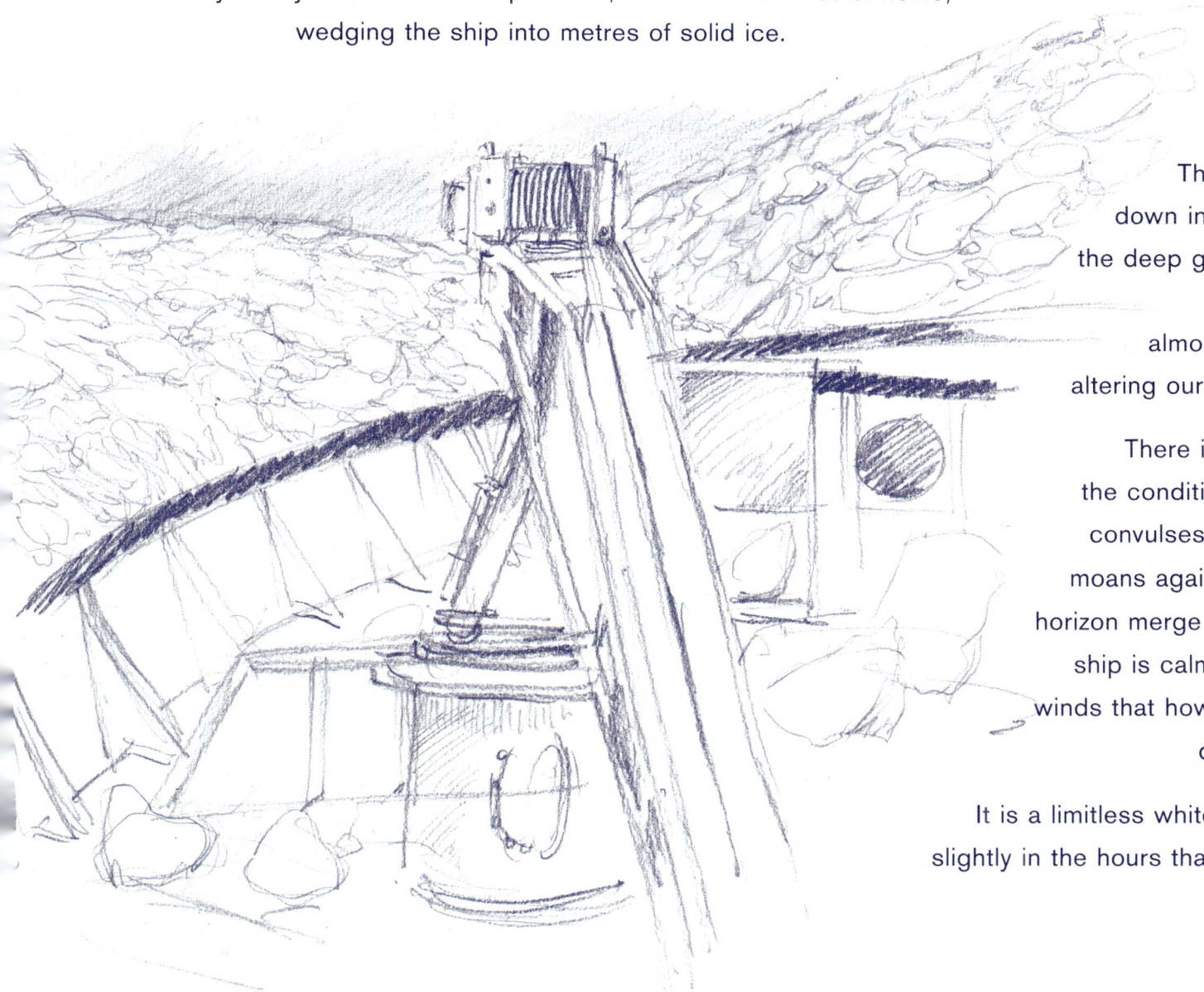

We secure everything and hold on as the captain turns the ship. The light darkens as the ship slides down into the bowels of the swell, inside the deep green-black depths of the ocean… then miraculously we are pushed, almost surfing the backs of the swells, altering our course for the safety of solid ice.

There is nothing we can do but wait out the conditions in this surreal landscape that convulses under us as the ice scrapes and moans against the ship. Low visibility and no horizon merge the sea and sky. One side of the ship is calm, the other is attacked by furious winds that howl at 50 knots through locked sea doors, screaming to an empty sky.

It is a limitless white – a cloak of light that only dims slightly in the hours that should be reserved for the dark.

And so, we wait.   **CT**

9

Going to Antarctica by ship has always been a hair-raising experience. In 1838, the explorer Jules Dumont d'Urville painted this picture of his ship in a storm, the sailors clinging on for dear life. **AL**

'I don't think anyone on the ship really expected to survive and, over a period of twelve hours, each roll seemed likely to be the last... Suddenly, struck by a fierce gust of wind and a particularly high wave, the ship heeled over until I was lying on my stomach on the bulkhead, practically horizontal with my nose flattened against the submerged glass of the porthole, gazing into the green-black depths. There I waited and waited for the recovery that would not come, as successive waves ground the ship further and further down on its side and my terror mounted. Finally after shaking and shuddering and deliberating, the vessel slowly moved back to position and I stood once again on the deck with pounding heart and sweat pouring down my back.' PHILLIP LAW, 1995

Each voyage awaits the sighting of the first berg
with excitement – confirmation the continent is coming and heralding
the entrance to an old, ancient world, seen new. **CT**

The first iceberg we saw was as big as a ten-storey building, and that's what we could see above the water. Ninety per cent of an iceberg is below the surface. It took about two hours to reach after we first saw it. We passed close enough to see that the base was like an icy beach. As the waves washed over, they turned pale turquoise and a lacy foam stretched and shifted with the tide.   **AL**

To voyage into the realm of Antarctica is a rite of passage.

The length of days expand. The temperature of the air and water decreases on an endless horizon of sky and ocean, often bleeding into each other seamlessly. You get used to riding the swells from inside the ship. Sometimes it is in graceful harmony with the flow beneath you, sometimes calling out against the strains and pull of currents as they swirl in a mass of power, sliding and crashing into erratic sets of waves – until the ice comes.

One day, you wake to understand what the ship is – a tiny dot of civilisation in a vast pool of water, in a never-ending, heaving, reflective blue landscape. The further south you voyage, the more you understand you need to submit to a new way of existing in the world around you.

You become used to the long days, the light erasing the darkness of night.

Ice crystals form like an oily, calming layer on the ocean's surface, until new ice, illuminated crystals, rustle and whisper at the side of the ship. The crystals freeze together, creating swirling pancake shapes, until they grow so large they merge, ice to ice, lying as a thick mass to the horizon.

The ice feels as if it has halted the nature of the sea. As your ship slices through its surface, it is your guide to this new world. **CT**

'The swells are like a sheet moving in a breeze, swells as beautiful as dunes in the Sahara.'
IREEN HOUBEN, 2023

'The solitude of the sea intensifies the thoughts and the facts of one's experience which seems to lie at the very centre of the world, as the ship which carries one always remains the centre figure of the round horizon.' JOSEPH CONRAD, 1913

As we sailed further south and our evenings lengthened, the ship's crew told me tales outside on the deck, as if these were bedtime stories just for me. One of these was about the Convergence.

The Convergence (or Polar Front as it is now named) is the place where the masses of cold and warm water and air meet each other. A wavy line, unpredictable on a map.

It was here, they said, that great clouds of mist were born from this confused meeting, forming a barrier to the south – sometimes benevolent, but also judgemental – but something that all ships must cross through. If voyages didn't meet with the lore of the sea, ships were said to have vanished through the clouds, never to be seen again.

I imagined great indigo clouds, brooding and expanding, showing some ethereal light from inside, a light to another world. But the clouds of my imagination never arrived.

The Convergence may not exist as they told me, may only live on in the tales of sailors: part warning, part fairytale. But there is a sense of entering another world, suspending known beliefs and living in a dream – one built of danger and difficulties, one of rare beauty and extraordinary humility – a place you can only visit, before returning to the known world as if you have been part of a story.   **CT**

Small pieces of brash ice,
like frozen chameleons, float
past as they change and melt in
warmer waters, away from the safety
of the pack.

An animated circus of fallen
cities and strange creatures create
a theatrical cast, performing their
last stories as they ride the ocean
currents northward.

The certificate reads:

Let it be Known that from the salty, salpy depths we rise to stir the wind, the stars and Ocean waves — to guide safe passage to the good ship RSV Nuyina. All who wish to cross the veil of the South must pay respect to the law of the Ocean — and stand before our maritime judgement.

I Australis Rex, ruler of the Southern Ocean — take the right to cast my eye upon all those of sodden feet who voyage through our Southern Realm — to land upon its icy shores.

It is declared that . . . . has paid humility and reverence to this passage and is found to be of sound and watery character.

So, it pleases us that the holder of this certificate be now dubbed a South Polar Sea Dog, to take pride in the brine that will course through their veins — And that this same South Polar Sea Dog be now Known as a true and trusted salt respecting all and from here on will call the snaggletooths and sea devils — friends.

Dated . . . .   Signed on behalf of — Australis Rex — by —

On the good ship RSV Nuyina

VOYAGE LEADER   MASTER

AUSTRALIAN ANTARCTIC PROGRAM

Neptune (Neptunus Rex) is the Roman god of the ocean and seas, who also controls the winds and storms. Some may see him as a fiction, a superstition – but respect for Neptune and his rules is taken very seriously on all ships. In the Southern Ocean, he is known as Australis Rex.

I created this certificate, with the help of Captain Gerry O'Doherty, for all who voyage south on Australia's icebreaker, RSV *Nuyina*.   **CT**

'I love the ceremony of making a fuss of crossing the Antarctic Circle. I sometimes think the ritual is not so much about the seafarer (or expeditioner) paying homage to King Neptune, but King Neptune acknowledging the newcomer to the Antarctic as an honourable person on a quest to do honourable work.'
CAPTAIN GERRY O'DOHERTY, 2023

We had a ceremony to celebrate crossing the Antarctic Circle. We had to bow to King Neptune, have a nasty mixture like porridge tipped on our heads, then kiss a stinky old fish head.   **AL**

SOUTH POLAR SEA DOG NAMES

A Neptune ceremony can also include giving each newly appointed sea dog a south polar name. Neptune's guards can give out these names, or one can be granted by throwing a dice and following the circles to choose a name.

Wheel 1 (centre): Fast · Frost smoke · Sundog · Sastrugi · Storm catcher · Opalescent · Floe · Cape · Crystal · Caldera · Earth shadow · Current · Lead · Frazil · Katabatic · Bay · Pancake · King · Fata Morgana · Sludge · Shore · Plunderfish · Under · Seal · Nilas · Neve · South · Cell · Mirage · Bubbly · Rookery · Toothfish · Frostbite · Grease

Wheel 2: Noctilucent · Tide crack · Rorqual · Firn · Weddell · Meteorite · Glacier · Minke · Granite · Slush · Spongy · Crabeater · Cliff · Antarctician · Prion · Salty · Nunatak · Gulf

Wheel 3: Emperor · Plateau · Barrier · Icy · Sei · Blubber · Gentoo · Sooty · Ele · Winter · Lid · Ross · Tafoni · Lightfish · King · Sleeper · Greywacke · Growler · Pole · Adélie · Brash

Wheel 4: Hoar frost · Crustacean · Fin · Phytoplankton · Wind-chill · Cloudy · Halo · Stinker · Berg · Snowy · Crevasse · Humpback · Pod · Snotsicle · Squid · Nelly · Frozen · Algae · Fossil

Wheel 5: Pod · Petrel · Summer · Big eye · Skua · Albatross · Sea · Scalyhead · Slushy · Sled · Lava · Shuga · Moondog · Diatom · Huddle · Whiteout · Whale · Echinoderm · Leopard · Krill

Wheel 6 (bottom centre): Stormy · Ice blink · Kelp · Scree · Wavy · Crusty · Polynya · Ocean

Wheel (lower left, 6): Aurora · Ozone · Blizzard · Snowbow · Colony · Slush · Bergy · Baleen

Wheel (lower right, 6): Tern · Orca · Moraine · Drift · Pressure · Moss · Royal · Pack

To voyage south was to voyage into the unknown, uncharted world.

In the Southern Ocean, there was once a group of nineteen islands, known as the non-existent Antarctic islands.

The lore of the sea demanded that it could be fatal not to chart an island that might exist, even if its reality was questionable, and all eyes were set to the horizon to keep watch for any new land.

Some islands may have been icebergs or clouds in the distance, some may have been due to the tired eyes and imaginations of sailors, but real or not, they existed on charts for many years. **CT**

High blue cliffs hung over us and chunks of ice that had fallen from them bobbed around the boat. We saw exquisite ice caves and grottos, with fringes of glittering stalactites hanging from their arches, the sea reflecting in dancing patterns of light across the turquoise ice.

The icebergs are so extraordinary that your imagination goes wild. You see pyramids, opera houses, ships, lions and castles. I half expected a frosty wizard to appear in one of the glowing blue caves.

The Russian artist Pavel Mikhailov sailed to Antarctica with the great explorer Thaddeus von Bellingshausen in 1820, and he turned the 'ice islands' into familiar things too. **AL**

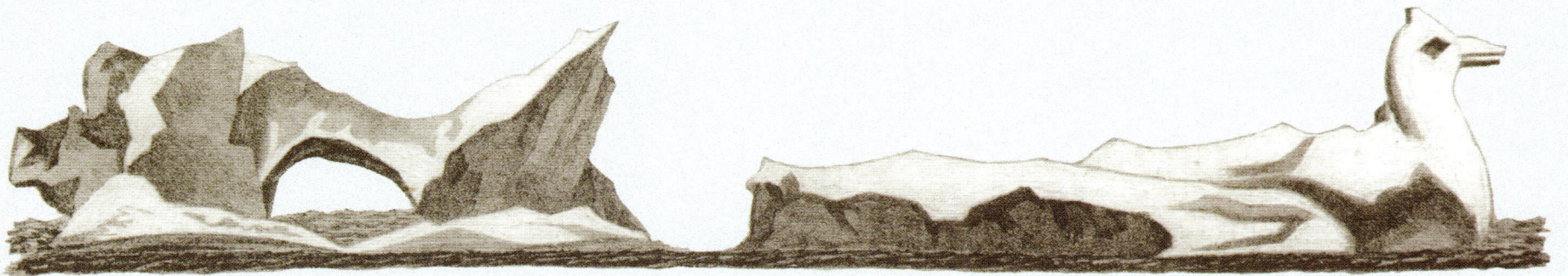

'Gazing at the grey curtains of fog from the deck of our ship, so tiny in the surrounding vastness, we felt like Argonauts whose quest had led us to the world's brim. Slowly we crept on, filled with wonder and expectancy ... through a rift we made out the glimmering sheen of a colossal berg.'

FRANK HURLEY, 1912

'I was staggered to find so much colour down there … the sky is often quite green, and the fringes of the icebergs and floes have a turquoise colouring. Sunsets are fantastic crimsons, oranges, golds and greens … I was frightened I'd miss something if I went to bed … Every hour there was something different to see and paint.' NEL LAW, 1961

'Krill are small but mighty. They help nature and people by storing carbon and helping maintain stable climatic conditions. They also power some of the largest animals on Earth like the majestic blue whale. Without these tiny ocean heroes, our biggest heroes couldn't survive.' EMILY GRILLY, 2023

'I found myself in the bowsprit of a six-metre boat in Antarctica next to a thirty-metre Antarctic blue whale, building up the courage to place a satellite tag on its flank. As the giant broke the surface, my mind went blank. I know I didn't even attempt to deploy that satellite tag. I was dumbstruck as a wall of blue just kept rising out of the ocean.

This is the beauty of working in the Southern Ocean. Not a day goes by that you don't wonder at the immensity of your surroundings and the animals and plants that inhabit that wild environment. And in turn, this wonder is the spark that ignites our passion, curiosity and drive to understand, conserve and protect this unique and incredible place.' VIRGINIA ANDREWS-GOFF, 2023

Some of the fish that swim in the sea,
below the ice and storms.

Marine Hatchet
and friend

Plunder
fish

Long fin
Icedevil

Daggertooth

Notothenia
antarctica

Bristlemouth

Toothfish

Ringed Barra

Characters of the deep.

Draco Rayado

Marine Hatchets

Snaggletooth

Ridgehead

Deep-sea Smelt

Cutthroat Eel

Seadevil

Patagonian toothfish

'You strange, astonished-looking, angle-faced,

Dreary-mouthed, gaping wretches of the sea,

Gulping salt-water everlastingly,

Cold-blooded, though with red your blood be graced,

And mute, though dwellers in the roaring waste'

LEIGH HUNT, 'To a Fish' (1836)

Drawn from nature by I. Weddell.

Sea Leopard of South Ork

I, Clark sculp.

I love this 'sea leopard' James Weddell drew in 1825. It's so fat and funny, and its head is so small. It's actually a Weddell seal, named after him. They are cumbersome on the ice, moaning and groaning as though they have stomach-aches, but under the ice they are sleek and graceful and make exquisite noises like an electronic orchestra. **AL**

The ship sliced through mirror-flat water, sun dazzling down, no breath of wind. Mount Erebus lay ahead, smoking. We had come through days of the wildest weather anybody on board had ever witnessed. The day felt like a gift, a reward for the passage we had endured.

Outside the porthole, something caught my eye. It was as though somebody had flung a handful of golden confetti into the blue sky. I looked again and saw the confetti was a flotilla of brown and white birds, the sun turning them gold, flying above the ship.

I raced up to the top deck and I was right among them. I could hear their wings beating. They were flying at the same speed as the ship, hundreds of them, escorting us into the Ross Sea. AL

'Large numbers of Antarctic petrels circled round and round the ship. Their numbers were so great that as the flights passed close by, the whirring of the wings could distinctly be heard on board.'
SIR ERNEST SHACKLETON, 1910

34

My heart skipped when I realised I was looking at mountains.

After weeks at sea, we had reached the continent.

Antarctica was real.   **AL**

'Above us the sun shone in a cloudless sky ... behind us lay the
lofty snow-clad mountains, the brown sun-kissed cliffs of the
Cape and the placid glassy waters of the bay ... it seemed
an atmosphere in which all Nature should rejoice ...'
CAPTAIN ROBERT F. SCOTT, 1905

'From the summits of these ice mountains many streams fed by the rapidly melting snows leapt down to the sea. All we could see were two menacing perpendicular walls beside us. When our eyes turned towards *Zelee*, following a short distance behind us, she looked so tiny, her rigging so frail, that we were unable to suppress a feeling of terror.' JULES DUMONT D'URVILLE, 1847

'Bergs and pack ice are thrown up and distorted into fantastic shapes…forming long and beautiful snow-cliffs, washed at their bases by the waters of illusion in which they appear faithfully reflected. In shore appears a beautiful dazzling city of cathedrals, spires, domes and minarets.'   FRANK WORSLEY, 1931

'The noise resembles the roar of heavy, distant surf. Standing on the stirring ice one can imagine it is disturbed by the breathing and tossing of a mighty giant below.'   SIR ERNEST SHACKLETON, 1919

'The ice was here, the ice was there,
The ice was all around:
It cracked and growled, and roared and howled,
Like noises in a swound!…
The ice did split with a thunder-fit;
The helmsman steered us through!…
And we did speak only to break
The silence of the sea!'
SAMUEL TAYLOR COLERIDGE,
'The Rime of the Ancient Mariner' (1798)

39

I couldn't help searching for something embedded
in the towering ice cliffs. Blue light seemed to come from
within the ice and every crack glowed. I imagined rocks,
huskies that fell down a crevasse a hundred years ago,
or the fossil of an ancient dinosaur.   **AL**

Emperor penguins are extremely dignified and composed. They seem to be aware of their incredible beauty, and pose regally to be admired. The comical Adélies always look flustered and unsure of where they're going. Seeing them together was like watching kids meet their football heroes. **AL**

'I can truthfully say that I had forgotten much of the outside world. My sense of values had so readjusted itself that for the time being I was unable to picture an existence in which a desert of ice and snow, battles with sea-leopards, the dread of killer-whales, and a great regard for penguins as almost personal friends did not play a part.'
FRANK WORSLEY, 1931

'Adelie penguins exhibit at times remarkable instincts and judgement; at other times their stupidity is almost incredible. Their pertinacity is exemplary, their curiosity ludicrous, and their bravery, amazing.'
HERBERT G. PONTING, 1921

44

'Antarctica has always been a special place because it is the home of the emperor penguins. These birds are miracles of evolution having managed to survive and thrive in the most inhospitable place on Earth. Emperors have been around for millennia and now the actions of one species may well be the end of them. Anthropogenic climate change is destroying their home, taking their food and possibly causing their extinction. To me it is inconceivable that although we know this, humanity appears unwilling or unable to change its way.' BARBARA WIENECKE, 2023

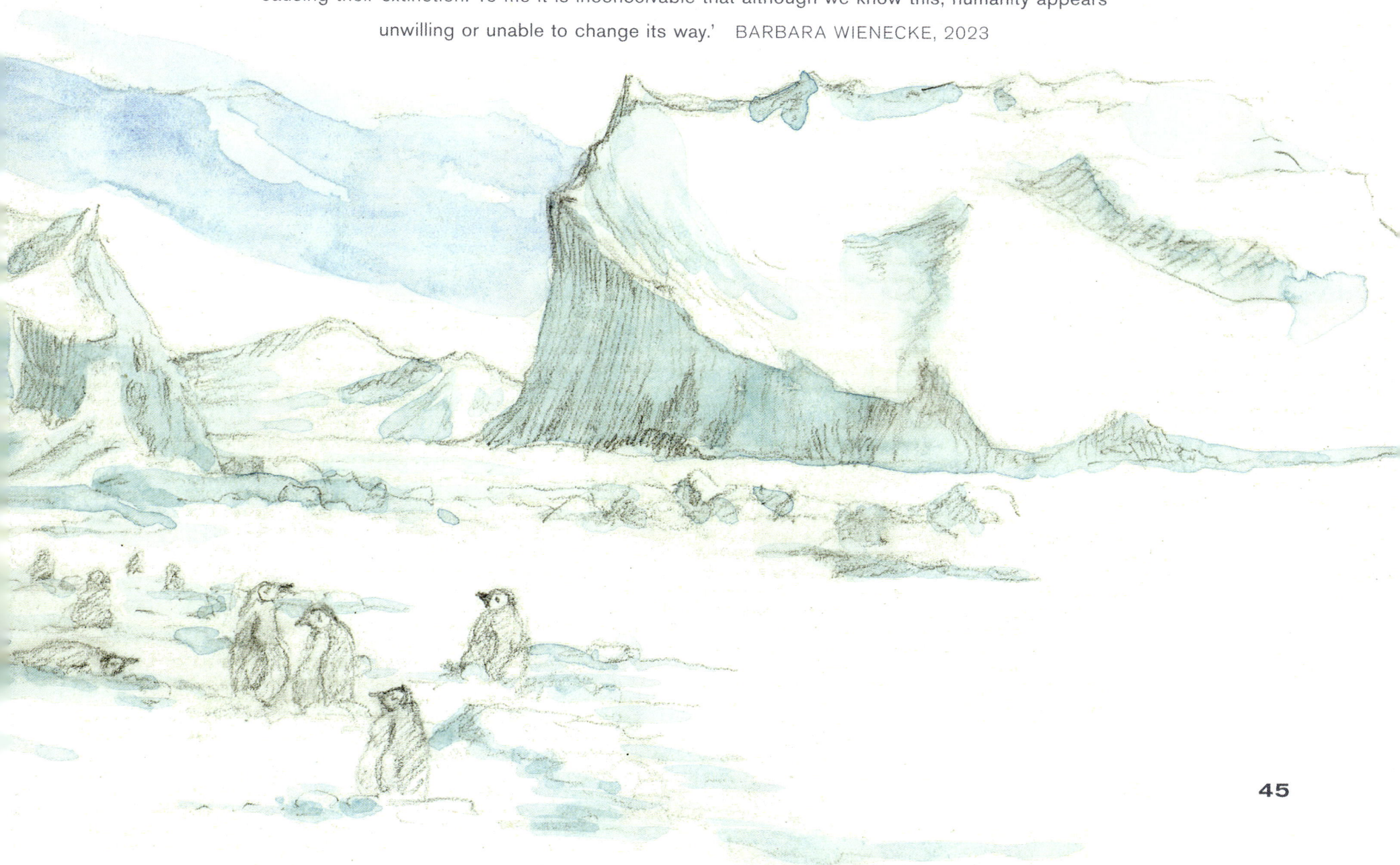

One morning, we woke to a white fog descending. We were close to Cape Washington but couldn't see the towering mountains surrounding us.

So much snow fell that day, a record according to some, an obvious consequence of climate change according to others.

A whiteout developed when even birds couldn't fly, as the frozen ocean, land and sky merged into one white veil. We waited, suspended in time, in a limbo, waiting for a glimpse of the world to return.

I wanted to translate what we were experiencing, but a photograph would have been just a scene of glaring white. Instead, I used a timeline and sketched what little I could see, using white squares on a black background to capture the story of the day.

It is said you cannot take a bad photograph in Antarctica, but this work shows how often you must wait – wait for the weather, wait to see where you are. **CT**

'The air is so pure and the light so clear that the distance runs to meet you, so details are once more seen with the clarity of younger eyes.'
JOHN DE LA ROCHE, 2023

'It spreads to all sides, an unbounded void of alien whiteness and geometric rigor, as though Charon, the icy moon of Pluto, had splashed softly to Earth.'
STEPHEN J. PYNE, 1986

46

9 am.

9.30am.

10 am.

10.30am.

11.00am.

11.30am.

12 noon.

12.30

13.00

13.30

14.00

14.30

15.00

15.30

16.00

16.30

48

Through the years of researching Antarctic material, I was stunned by the voices that arose from many of the early expeditioners, not known previously for their poetic natures. One of my favourites was Dr Edward Wilson, whose sublime landscapes mapped the unknown and brought the romance of Antarctica to a world that he would never return to. I found myself, unconsciously, drawing long vistas, inspired by the legacy he left for us all.   **CT**

I walked alone towards the mountains, the spiky chains

on my boots clattering on the ice. It was absolutely freezing cold and I was tiny and

alone in that vast landscape with no shelter, completely at the mercy of the elements.

When I turned around, I could see the ship way, way down in the harbour and the

buildings around the bay, and they were tiny as well.   **AL**

'Nowhere are words so obviously ineffectual a response

to what just, massively, exists, whole and complete and in

no real need of translation. Words, Antarctica teaches us,

are not what the world is made of…Step aside…

Sit for a while…Take a long, silent look at the treasures

of the snow.' FRANCIS SPUFFORD, 2008

In this place where our known perceptions are altered, where every sense

we possess and have long trusted is challenged and changed dramatically,

you have to find a new way to express what you are seeing and feeling.

Time is measured in the thickness of an ice sheet and language is awkward and foreign.

Some cannot describe what they are experiencing. Many are silent for a long time,

as if they are searching for a new common language.   **CT**

The Antarctic atmosphere is like a great theatre,

projecting strange mirages of floating icebergs and capturing haloes of light.

Sun dogs illuminate icebergs, like sentinels, columns at the entrance to a separate reality.   **CT**

'When the sun was out there were nearly always mock-suns red or gold or prismatic and always

magnificent ... When you gazed upon this strange and awe-inspiring sky you felt as though you had stepped into

a world where the laws of Nature, as you had known them, were suspended and over-ruled by some vast Power,

which was thus making itself known to you.' FRANK WORSLEY, 1931

An aurora stretched across the sky, shimmering and dancing in front of the stars. It swooped right over us in a wide band of neon green, then finished with a swirl. **AL**

'To the south there appeared two columns of a whitish-blue colour similar to phosphorescent fire, flashing from clouds along the horizon with the rapidity of rockets. Each column was as broad as three diameters of the sun ... Sometimes across the whole of the sky there were feathers of light ...' CAPTAIN THADDEUS VON BELLINGSHAUSEN, 1820

The landscape slides away from you in depth and height

so that the horizon seems an unreachable dream.

Clouds spin with opalescent colours, the ocean's waves suspend their flight in frost, each crystal reflecting a rainbow, and ancient atmosphere is trapped inside blue ice that weighs down the land, the continent. It is as if secrets of the Earth are hidden in the folds of snow, just out of reach, and with respect and awe you tread carefully, trying to understand this new world and learn its rhythms. **CT**

It looked as though the mountains were poking up through mist, but as we drew closer, we could see that it was ice. The jagged mountain range, ancient spires of grey rock, sat in a bed of ice thousands of metres thick. 'Nunatak' means lonely mountain in Inuit languages. We are used to seeing mountains with ice and snow on their peaks, but here, the order was reversed.   **AL**

Away from the coast, the plateau rises up as a cloak of ice. Nunataks defy the weight of ice and time to show their peaks. There is no life apart from the constant frozen wind, sculpting the rock and ice, and the strain of ice as it moves and cracks against itself. It is so silent that you can hear your pulse, and so dry that when you walk on rocks, they can tinkle like fairies' bells. **CT**

When I walked out into a dwindling blizzard at Mawson Station, I wore layers and layers of polar clothes but I was still freezing. It's hard to imagine how the expeditioners of the heroic age survived in the clothing they had. Some of them looked to the Arctic and copied the furs that the people wore there, but the British mostly stuck with wool and gabardine. They must have been freezing.

They lost fingers and toes to frostbite, starved, went snow-blind, their teeth cracked, their lips split, and the soles of Douglas Mawson's feet fell off.

The tents were small cotton and bamboo pyramids, designed to withstand gales. Sleeping bags were reindeer hide, with the fur on the inside. Any small drop of perspiration turned to ice in these bags and they soon became stiff, icy envelopes that couldn't even be rolled up. **AL**

'The English have loudly and openly told the world that ski and dogs are unusable in these regions and that fur clothes are rubbish. We will see – we will see.' ROALD AMUNDSEN, 1911

'December 21 – Midsummer Day … We have frostbitten fingers and ears, and a strong blizzard wind has been blowing from the south all day … Our beards are masses of ice all day long.' SIR ERNEST SHACKLETON, 1908

'I do not believe any man, however sick he is, has a much worse time than we had in those bags, shaking with cold until our backs would almost break.' APSLEY CHERRY-GARRARD, 1922

Twenty-two men stayed on Elephant Island while Shackleton and five others sailed a lifeboat, the *James Caird*, through perilous seas for help. They lived under two upturned lifeboats for four-and-a-half months, through an Antarctic winter, surviving on penguins and seals. This drawing is based on George Marston's painting of The Snuggery, as they called it.

It was a filthy space, black with soot from the blubber stove. Reindeer hair from the sleeping bags mixed with smoke, and the men and their clothes reeked as there was no way of washing. They slept packed together like smoked sardines and snored like elephant seals. **AL**

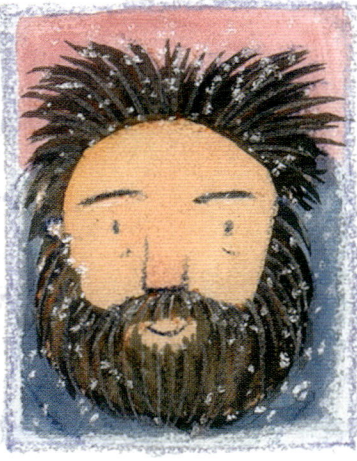

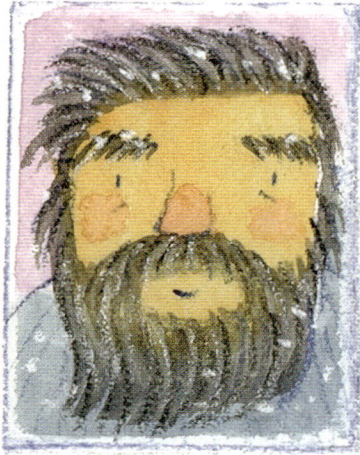

Many of the explorers loved the ponies and dogs like friends. It must have been heartbreaking when they had to say goodbye to them. Dr Edward Wilson fed all his meagre rations to his pony Nobby as he struggled to pull a sled through deep snow, and Harry McNish never forgave Shackleton for ordering his cat, Mrs Chippy (here with the stowaway Perce Blackborow) to be shot before they took to the lifeboats. **AL**

'[Tom] Crean had started to take the pups out for runs, and it was very amusing to see them with their rolling canter just managing to keep abreast by the sledge and occasionally cocking an eye with an appealing look in the hope of being taken aboard for a ride.'

SIR ERNEST SHACKLETON, 1911

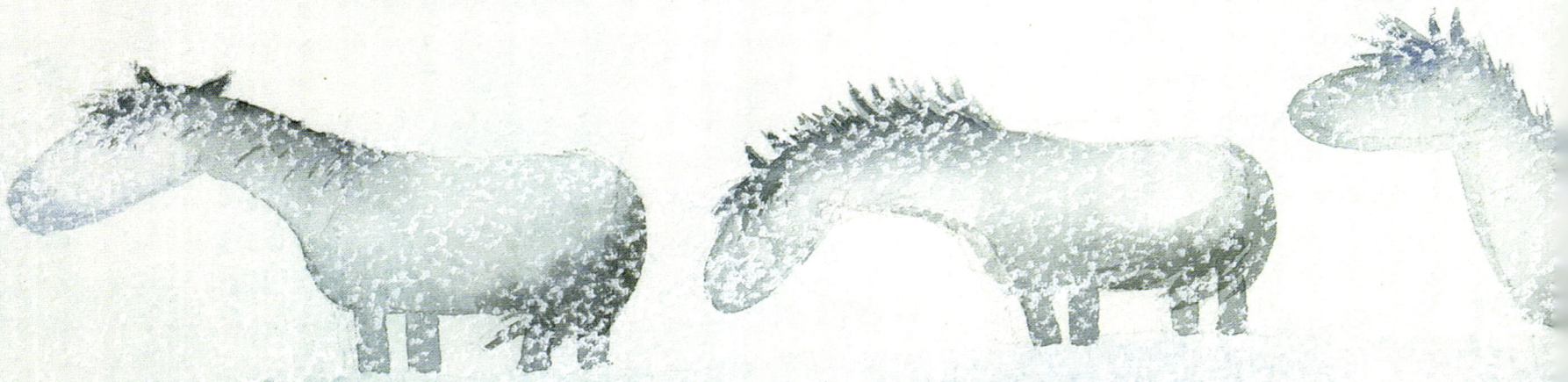

The explorers' huts were their refuge, a tiny place of warmth and nourishment in the home of the blizzard. They must have driven each other crazy at times, squashed together, all those different personalities.

Robert F. Scott was desperate for his *Terra Nova* expedition to be first to the South Pole. When I stood in his hut at Cape Evans, I imagined the sad, dark winter months the men spent there, waiting for the ship to come in spring, knowing Scott and the others had perished on the way back from the pole. **AL**

'That strong little house, that now lay entirely hidden beneath the snow behind Mount Nelson, had for a whole year been our home, and a thoroughly good and comfortable home it was, where after so many a hard day's work we had found all the rest and quiet we wanted.' ROALD AMUNDSEN, 1912

Roald Amundsen was determined to beat Scott to the pole. He arrived in Antarctica and he built his hut, Framheim, on the ice shelf, to be closer to the South Pole. When the hut became buried in snow, the party dug a series of rooms and workshops with tunnels that connected them to the main building.

Amundsen reached the South Pole in December 1911 and got back to Framheim in January. Five days later they sailed away, leaving their home, with just its chimney poking up.

When that chunk of the ice shelf broke away last century, Framheim was adrift, buried in an iceberg. **AL**

As the ice melted, Amundsen's hut would have
emerged and drifted around the Southern Ocean, until the
berg melted away and the hut sank into the sea.

Did anybody see it? Perhaps an albatross as she soared around the world.
Maybe the sun reflected on the windows and gave the appearance of a light
shining from within. And possibly a wisp of cloud drifted past the chimney
as though a hearty fire was roaring below.   **AL**

When the *Endurance* was beset then crushed, and sank beneath the ice in the Weddell Sea in 1914, Shackleton and his team were stranded on the sea ice, with no hope of rescue.

Theirs is one of the most famous survival stories in history: not a man lost after a year and a half.

Incredibly, in 2022, more than one hundred years after she sank, the wreck of the *Endurance* was discovered on the seabed, preserved by the icy Antarctic seawater. **AL**

'A strange occurrence was the sudden appearance of eight emperor penguins from a crack 100 yds. away at the moment the pressure on the ship was at its climax. They walked a little way towards us, halted, and after a few ordinary calls proceeded to utter weird cries that sounded like a dirge for the ship. None of us had ever before heard the emperors utter any other than the most simple calls or cries, and the effect of this concerted effort was almost startling.' SIR ERNEST SHACKLETON, 1913

There is a long history in Antarctica of people taking something with them that reminds them of home, or something they love. Whatever it is, it's a deeply personal connection for them to the world outside Antarctica, a connection with the familiar in a place so unfamiliar, so far from home.

On the ship *Terra Nova*, Frank Debenham's teddy sits on the table in the Wardroom, with its arm waving to the camera.   **CT**

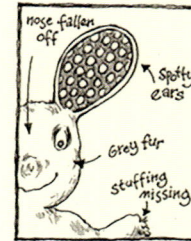

Sydney, a family treasure, was taken on a voyage to Antarctica.
Placed on a rock for a photograph, he was mistakenly left behind at Cape Evans.

Time in Antarctica is measured in light and dark, and as we know, toys do not understand time.
So, as the constant sunshine passes into constant darkness and back again,
it would seem like only days for a little mouse on an adventure.

Over the years, many have searched for Sydney and this poster still exists to help find him. The ice can reveal secrets and one day he will be found. For now, it's believed he still has much more to do. **CT**

Leaving the continent is to leave the ice, and leaving the ice can be traumatic.

For some, there is a sense of loss, a pain so deep that they become quiet and withdrawn. As the voyage heads further north, they can no longer refuse the fact that the air is getting warmer, and that the world they knew is coming back to them. Friends and family await. Work and the combined, layered chaos of centuries of human toil and noise will soon surround them.

Leaving the ice, again – the silence is pronounced. Once again, language is foreign.

In the days of early exploration, the hardships, constant work and worry of the expeditions would have made many scars that could not be healed, soothed only by the approach of the homeward-bound ship. But many from that era are reported to have longed to go back, and did.

Once you leave Antarctica, as the power of the ocean fluidly speeds you home, you can smell the salt of the sea and the first land, but the longing for the ice stays in your dreams. **CT**

'The cold ice no longer sleeps below,
Above a warming sky now expands,
And all around
With a fiery sound,

Gone has the ice and melted the snow
The heat of climate change does quickly flow
From our human hands.'
DR PETRA HEIL, 'Fire' (2023), after 'The cold earth
slept below' (1823) by Percy Bysshe Shelley

81

The last iceberg always takes you by surprise because while you're in the ice, you take the wonder of it for granted. Suddenly you realise you are passing the last iceberg and you may never, ever see an iceberg again. The fantastic, beautiful world you've been in, that wild time of ice, is over. **AL**

AUCKLAND IS

MOTU MAHA / MAUNGAHUKA

ÎLE AMSTERDAM

ÎLE ST-PAUL

MARION IS

PRINCE EDWARD IS

In the sub-Antarctic, where the great oceans of the world melt into the vast Southern Ocean, tiny tips of land rise up and push against the waves. Voyaging south, they are

BOUNTY ISLANDS
Moutere Hauriri
Marine Reserve

ANTIPODES IS
Moutere Mahue Marine Reserve

SOUTH SHETLAND ISLANDS

BALLENY ISLANDS

POSSESSION ISLANDS

ELEPHANT IS

CAMPBELL IS / MOTU IHUPUKU

SOUTH GEORGIA

ÎLE

sentinels to the Antarctic, a nursery for animals and birds. Voyaging north they are a farewell to the ice, a reminder of green lands and the scent of the world beyond.

FALKLAND ISLANDS
ISLAS MALVINAS

SOUTH

ORKNEY ISLANDS

PETER 1ØY

MACQUARIE IS

COULMAN IS

SOUTH SANDWICH ISLANDS

BOUVETØYA

SCOTT IS

GOUGH IS
Conçalo Álvares

OZET

McDONALD IS

HEARD IS

ÎLES KERGUELEN

THE SNARES
TINI HEKE

Stormy seas took us to the sub-Antarctic islands and seasickness kept the dining room empty. I woke up one morning and realised the ship was not moving. It was a shock to look out the porthole and see a green hill. The island was teeming with seals, penguins and birds. It's where many animals come to breed and raise their young, this halfway house to Antarctica. **AL**

'Those days in the Antarctic when your little ship's driving through blinding snow, ice, icebergs, darkness and an angry sea, are days of deep anxiety... But it is not all gloom... especially when the sun shines forth with great brilliancy... upon those majestic peaks of eternal snow, and you gaze with feelings of indescribable delight upon a scene of grandeur and magnificence beyond anything you have seen or could have conceived.' LOUIS BERNACCHI, 1901

'The commonality of our endeavour, and the close working relationships we have, bring us together as a very close, bonded community. It is very special to be away in such a remote and incredible environment as the Antarctic and Southern Ocean with our small band of voyagers. It's truly the stuff of adventure stories and history.' CAPTAIN GERRY O'DOHERTY, 2023

'The primary reason Antarctica is important to me can be viewed as both a fact and an idea. That there are vast areas of Earth with inhabitants that don't encounter Homo sapiens on a day to day basis. Generations of penguins that never see people, crabeater seals that never see ships and valleys that never have footprints. A place that actually exists but also rests gently in the mind and heart. A place that can be visited by anyone's imagination. But alas our tentacles for damage and destruction creep ever closer to this paradise.' DR DANA BERGSTROM, 2023

'My encounters with and in Antarctica have impacted me in so many ways. The ethereal beauty creeps into my soul and silence prevails, except for the crunching sound of my boots on the frozen ocean. I felt an immediate connection with the Antarctic, and this love deepened with every passing day. I was drawn in and enchanted, knowing that I must teach others about this icy realm so they might love it too, and protect it as much as possible. The weight of environmental responsibility is heavy on my heart.' BETTY TRUMMEL, 2023

I grew up overlooking the sea in southern Australia, and Antarctica felt like a myth. It seemed unbelievable that there was a frozen continent far beyond the horizon. The epic journey there by ship, literally travelling to the end of the Earth, was a wild ride that I loved. Every day brought something new and incredible and I felt very lucky to be there. That adventurous joy, the completely different world, the vastness – it's all stayed with me as a reminder to treat the world as well as I can.

ALISON LESTER

Where else in the world can you walk among animals that are not afraid of you, where the goodness and generosity of people, in a society that is egalitarian and without pretence, is written into the law? It lingers from the heroic tales of the past and will continue to the future.

In our limited human visitation of this rare continent, we have been able to create a real social utopia and work to understand and protect this pristine environment. Where else in the world do all nations work together in peace and co-operation and war is banned?

The rules have been made by the environment, not humans changing the environment, but humbled by it, living by its rules.

Antarctica is not owned by one nation, but belongs to us all.

In these fragile times where we have changed so much of the natural world, and our planet is suffering the consequences of climate change, it is now so urgent that we must work together, to help understand and protect this continent to help our world survive.

CORAL TULLOCH

Amundsen, Roald (1872–1928)

Quotations on pp. 62 and 70 from *The South Pole: An Account of the Norwegian Antarctic Expedition in the 'Fram' 1910–1912* (1913) by Roald Amundsen, translated by Arthur G. Chater. Public domain.

Mentioned on pp. 71–73.

Roald Amundsen was a Norwegian polar explorer. He is famous for being the first person to lead an expedition to reach the South Pole, in December 1911.

Andrews-Goff, Dr Virginia

Quotation on p. 29. Used with permission.

Virginia Andrews-Goff is a Senior Marine Mammal Research Scientist at the Australian Antarctic Division.

Barnett, Susan

Image on p. 2. Used with permission.

Susan Barnett is a visual artist and author.

Bellingshausen, Captain Thaddeus von (1778–1852)

Quotation on p. 57 from *The Voyage of Captain Bellingshausen to the Antarctic Seas, 1819–1821* (2011). Translated from Russian. Edited by Frank Debenham. Published by Hakluyt Society. Used with permission from David Higham Associates Ltd.

Thaddeus von Bellingshausen was a Russian explorer, famous for his circumnavigation of Antarctica.

Bergstrom, Dr Dana

Quotation on p. 89. Used with permission.

Dana Bergstrom is an Antarctic ecologist.

Bernacchi, Louis (1876–1942)

Quotation on p. 88 from *To the South Polar Regions: Expedition of 1898–1900* (1901) by Louis Bernacchi. Public domain.

Louis Bernacchi was an Australian physicist and astronomer who travelled to Antarctica twice.

Blackborow, Perce (1896–1949)

In image on p. 66. Photo by Frank Hurley. Public domain.

Perce Blackborow was the youngest crew member of the *Endurance*. He stowed away on the ship in Buenos Aires.

Byrd, Admiral Richard E. (1888–1957)

Quotation on p. iv from *Alone: The Classic Polar Adventure* (1938) by Richard E. Byrd. Copyright © 1938 by Richard E. Byrd, renewed 1966 by Marie A. Byrd. Afterword Copyright © 2003 by Kieran Mulvaney. Reproduced by permission of Island Press, Washington, DC.

Richard E. Byrd was a US naval officer who was a pioneering aviator and polar explorer. He organised many successful expeditions to Antarctica.

Chambers, Justin

Image on pp. 56–57. Image copyright © Justin Chambers/Australian Antarctic Division.

Chef, Mawson Station, 2024, Australian Antarctic Territory.

Cherry-Garrard, Apsley (1886–1959)

Quotation on p. 62 from *The Worst Journey in the World: Antarctica 1910–1913* by Apsley Cherry-Garrard (1922). Public domain.

Apsley Cherry-Garrard was one of the youngest members of the *Terra Nova* expedition to Antarctica, where he served as an assistant zoologist.

Coleridge, Samuel Taylor (1772–1834)

Quotation on p. 39 from 'The Rime of the Ancient Mariner' (1798) by Samuel Taylor Coleridge. Public domain.

Samuel Taylor Coleridge was an early 1800s poet and philosopher.

Conrad, Joseph (1857–1924)

Quotation on p. 15 from *Chance* (1913) by Joseph Conrad. Public domain.

Joseph Conrad was a Polish-British novelist. His seafaring career led him to be praised for his gift for depicting life at sea and where it leads.

Crean, Tom (1877–1938)

In image on p. 67. Photo by Frank Hurley. Public domain.

Tom Crean was an Irish sailor who worked on three major Antarctic expeditions, including the *Terra Nova* expedition in 1911.

Debenham, Frank (1883–1965)

Mentioned on p. 76.

Frank Debenham was an Australian Antarctic geographer and scientist on the *Terra Nova* expedition.

Dumont d'Urville, Jules Sébastien César (1790–1842)

Quotation on p. 38 from *From Venus to Antarctic: The Life of Dumont d'Urville* (2007) by John Dunmore. Used with permission from Exisle Publishing.

Jules Dumont d'Urville was a French explorer with particular interest in botany. He explored Australia, New Zealand and Antarctica.

Emerson, Ralph Waldo (1803–1882)

Quotation on p. 6 from 'Wealth' in *The Conduct of Life* (1860) by Ralph Waldo Emerson. Public domain.

Ralph Waldo Emerson was an American poet, essayist, and philosopher.

Grilly, Emily

Quotation on p. 26. Used with permission.

Emily Grilly is a marine biologist and the Antarctic Conservation Manager at WWF-Australia.

Heil, Dr Petra

Quotation on p. 81. Used with permission.

Petra Heil is an earth-systems scientist.

Houben, Ireen

Quotation on p. 15. Used with permission.

Ireen Houben is a journalist and broadcaster.

Hume, Clair

Photograph on front endpaper. Used with permission.

Clair Hume is a writer, editor and publisher.

Hume, Edwin

Photographs on pp. 87 and 91. Used with permission.

Edwin Hume is a lawyer.

Hunt, Leigh (1784–1859)

Quotation on p. 31 from 'To a Fish' (1836) by Leigh Hunt. Public domain.

James Henry Leigh Hunt was a poet, critic and essayist.

Hurley, Frank (1885–1962)

Quotation on p. 22 from *Argonauts of the South: Being a Narrative of Voyagings and Polar Seas and Adventures in the Antarctic with Sir Douglas Mawson and Sir Ernest Shackleton* (1925) by Frank Hurley. Used with permission from Penguin Random House.

Images on pp. 22, 63, 66, 67 and 75.

James Francis 'Frank' Hurley was the official photographer for Douglas Mawson's 1913 Antarctic expedition and Ernest Shackleton's 1914 Trans-Antarctic Expedition.

Hussey, Leonard (1891–1964)

In image on p. 67. Photo by Frank Hurley.

Leonard Hussey was an English explorer, archaeologist, meteorologist and doctor on the Trans-Antarctic Expedition.

Law, Dr Phillip (1912–2010)

Quotation on p. 11 from *You have to be lucky: Antarctic and other adventures* by Phillip Law (1995).

Phillip Law was an Australian scientist and explorer who was the head of Australian National Antarctic Research Expeditions from 1949 to 1966. He personally led 23 expeditions to the continent.

Law, Nel (1914–1990)

Quotation on p. 23 from *Australian Women's Weekly*, 'Art in the Antarctic' (1961) by Sheila McFarlane. Copyright © Australian Women's Weekly. Used with permission.

Image on p. 23.

Nel Law was an artist and the first Australian woman to visit Antarctica, smuggled onto her husband Phillip's voyage in 1961.

Marston, George (1882–1940)

Painting on p. 74 titled: *The Endurance Crushed in the Ice of the Weddell Sea, October 1915*. Reproduced with the help of Bridgeman Images.

Artwork on p. 63 by Alison Lester inspired by *Drawing of men camping under a boat, the Snuggery, on Elephant Island*, by George Marston, composite with photograph by Frank Hurley.

George Marston was an English painter who accompanied Sir Ernest Shackleton on two of his Antarctic expeditions.

Mawson, Sir Douglas (1882–1958)

Mentioned on p. 62.

Douglas Mawson was an Australian Antarctic explorer and geologist. He was a part of the *Nimrod* expedition with Shackleton in 1907, and led Australia's first major scientific expedition, the Australian Antarctic Expedition in 1911.

McCall, Nigel

Photographs on pp. 33, 34–35, 70, 86–87, 90. Used with permission.

Nigel McCall is a photographer.

McNish, Henry (1874–1930)

Mentioned on p. 66.

Henry McNish, also known as Harry or 'Mr Chippy', was a Scottish carpenter on the *Endurance* expedition in 1914.

SOURCES

Mikhailov, Pavel (1786–1840)

Images on pp. 21 and 57. Used with permission from the State Historical Museum of Russia.

Mentioned on p. 20.

Pavel Mikhailov was the official artist on the first Russian expedition to the Southern Ocean, led by Thaddeus von Bellingshausen.

O'Doherty, Captain Gerry

Quotations on pp. 18 and 88.

Gerry O'Doherty was a captain of the 'farewelled' RSV *Aurora Australis* and now is a captain of the RSV *Nuyina*.

Papps, Wayne (1959–2003)

Images on pp. 55, 59 and 88–89. Images copyright © Wayne Papps/Australian Antarctic Division. Used with permission.

Wayne Papps was a wilderness photographer who was well-loved among the Australian Antarctic Division community, and returned with legendary photographs.

Ponting, Herbert G. (1870–1935)

Quotation on p. 42 from *The Great White South: being an account of experiences with Captain Scott's South Pole expedition and of the nature life of the Antarctic* (1922) by Herbert G. Ponting. Public domain.

Photographs on pp. 70 and 76.

Herbert G. Ponting was best known for his photography, writing and filming of Captain Robert F. *Scott's Terra Nova* expedition to Antarctica from 1910–1913.

Pyne, Stephen J.

Quotation on p. 46 from 'The Sheet' from *The Ice: A journey to Antarctica* (1986) by Stephen J. Pyne. Copyright © University of Washington Press.

Stephen J. Pyne was a professor at Arizona State University, specialising in environmental history. He is also the author of many books.

Roche, John de la

Quotation on p. 46. Used with permission.

John de la Roche is a photographer.

Scott, Captain Robert F. (1868–1912)

Quotation on p. 36 from *The Voyage of the Discovery, Volume 1* (1905) by Captain Robert F. Scott. Public domain.

Mentioned on pp. 70–71.

Robert F. Scott was a Royal Navy officer who explored Antarctica extensively in the 1900s, and died on his return trip from the South Pole in 1911.

Shackleton, Sir Ernest (1874–1922)

Quotations on pp. 34, 39, 62, 67 and 75 from *The Heart of the Antarctic* (1909) and *South! the story of Shackleton's last expedition 1914–1917* (1919) by Ernest Shackleton. Public domain.

Mentioned on pp. 63, 66 and 75.

Ernest Shackleton was a mariner and became famous for his Antarctic exploration. After the *Endurance* was crushed by ice, his leadership proved legendary in getting all his men to safety.

Spufford, Francis

Quotation on p. 52 from *The Antarctic* edited by Francis Spufford (2008). Published by Granta Books. Reproduced with permission from Granta Books.

Francis Spufford is an author and editor of both fiction and non-fiction books.

Trummel, Betty

Quotation on p. 89.

Betty Trummel is a polar educator.

Weddell, James (1787–1834)

Image on pp. 32–33. Courtesy of Linda Hall Library of Science, Engineering & Technology.

James Weddell was a British explorer and seal hunter, commanding three Antarctic voyages.

Weinecke, Dr Barbara

Quotation on p. 45. Used with permission.

Barbara Wienecke is a senior research scientist.

Wilson, Dr Edward (1872–1912)

Images on pp. 48 and 55. Courtesy of the Scott Polar Research Institute.

Mentioned on pp. 49 and 66.

Edward Wilson was a doctor, painter, natural historian and scientist. He was on the ill-fated expedition to the South Pole, along with Scott, Bowers and Oates, whose bodies still lie in the ice of Antarctica.

Worsley, Frank (1872–1943)

Quotations on pp. 39, 42 and 54 from *Endurance: An Epic of Polar Adventure* (1931) by Frank Worsley. Public domain.

Frank Worsley was a New Zealand sailor most famously remembered as the captain on Shackleton's *Endurance* expedition.

LIST OF IMAGES

ACKNOWLEDGEMENTS

We gratefully acknowledge the incredible support of the Australian Antarctic Division, for our time as Antarctic Arts Fellows and their continued support over the decades with all our projects. There are so many people who have been important to us, have inspired us and travelled with us. They are our Antarctic friends who share our love for and interest in this extraordinary continent. We thank them all as they are all a part of our journey.

Antarctic Heritage Trust New Zealand
Aurora Expeditions
Australian Antarctic Division
Barbara Frankel
Barbara Wienecke
Betty Trummel
Clair Hume
Dana Bergstrom
Danielle Hodder
Edwin Hume
Emily Grilly
Gerry O'Doherty
Gordon Bain
Ireen Houben
Jess Fitzpatrick, Creative Director, Australian Antarctic Division
John de la Roche
Nigel McCall
Petra Heil
Quark Expeditions
Robert Headland
Rod Ledingham
Sachie Yasuda
Stephen Eastaugh
Sue Barnett
Tess Eagen, Librarian, Australian Antarctic Division
The Scott Polar Institute
Tim Last
Virginia Andrews-Goff

First published by Allen & Unwin in 2024

Allen & Unwin
Cammeraygal Country
83 Alexander Street
Crows Nest NSW 2065
Australia
Phone: (61 2) 8425 0100
Email: info@allenandunwin.com
Web: www.allenandunwin.com

Allen & Unwin acknowledges the Traditional Owners of the Country on which we live and work. We pay our respects to all Aboriginal and Torres Strait Islander Elders, past and present.

A catalogue record for this book is available from the National Library of Australia

ISBN 978 1 76052 606 1

For teaching resources, explore allenandunwin.com/learn

Cover and text design by Sandra Nobes
Set in 12 pt Akzidenz-Grotesk Pro
This book was printed in June 2024 by 1010 Printing Limited, China

10 9 8 7 6 5 4 3 2 1

MIX
Paper | Supporting responsible forestry
FSC® C016973

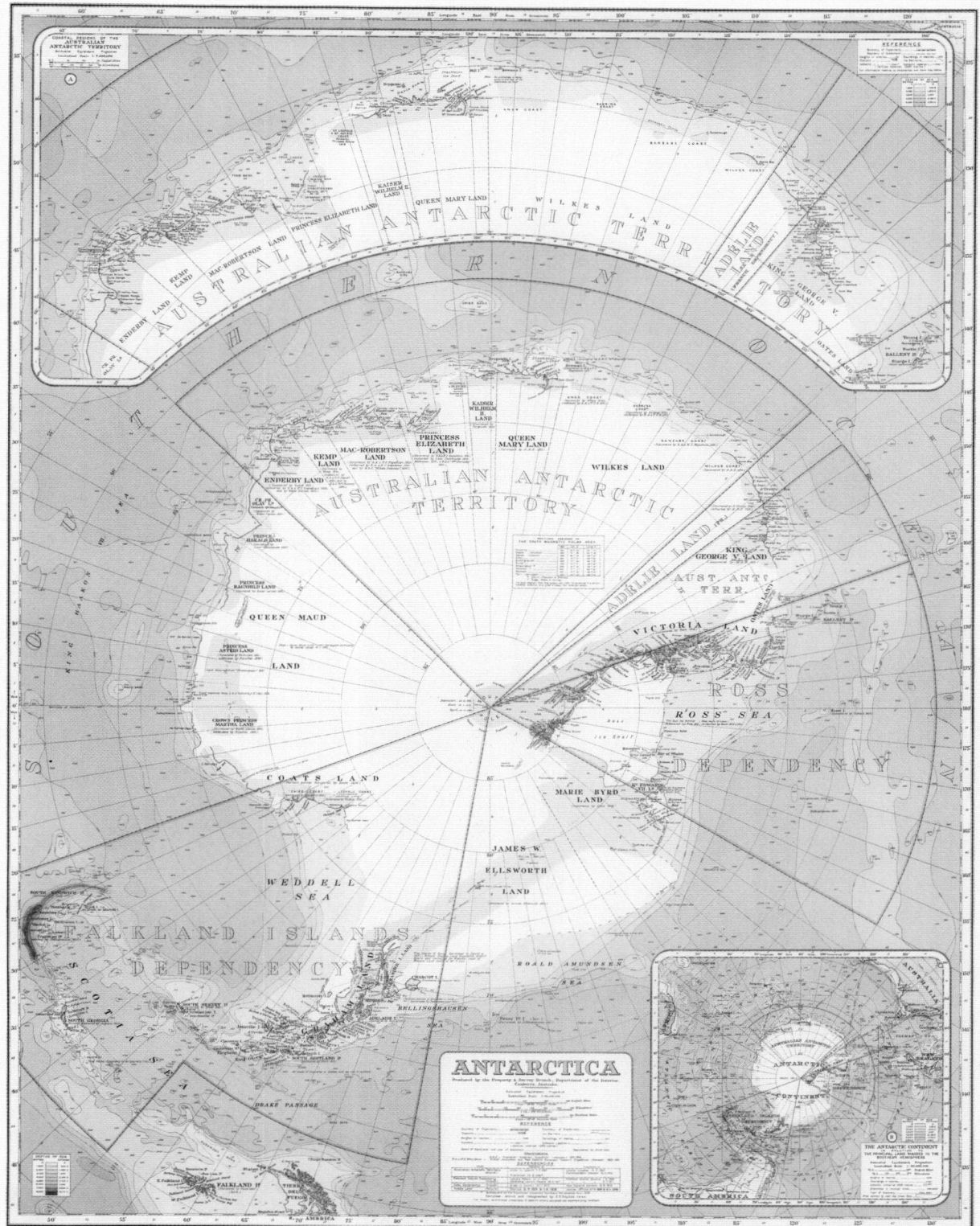